Lament for Us All

Lament for Us All

poems

Carlos Reyes

CONTENTS

II.   *Hoofprint on an Echo*

I.

Solitude

A Pandemic Prompt

On this another August
pandemic morning

my cloth mask
is covered with writing.

As I draw it close
the only legible line

comes into focus:
This island has no port.

The Last Time We Wore Masks

At nightfall no moon, no stars
but mud falling from the sky
between rain drops, until it landed

dried to sparkling, glassy sand
heavy ash a gift from Mt St Helens
50 miles away, half a life ago. Uninvited

guest with us day after day
too heavy to be washed away yet
was rising swirls of clouds behind

speeding cars. We raced through
the dusty wind, which
choked carburetors, choked us.

We didn't stay indoors
wear masks, we survived we're
here most of us, the ash is

a dim memory, subtle reminder

of violence, eruptions. Now rarely

found, it joined humus and duff

enriches the soil of our gardens.

Sometimes in deep woods

it still dusts fir boughs grey snow

or drifts behind a log on a stream

thread in the foothills it hides.

Even today an ignored remnant,

grains of some unread codicil

from deep beneath the earth.

– 1980

Quarantine

I.

During this pandemic

it's not so much that we're

prisoners in a cell

behind bars. It's more

like being kept in by

rays of light we can't see,

invisible death and off and on

wrinkles of fear, afraid to talk, to

embrace our children, friends.

II.

Unlike the whooping cough

quarantine of the 1930s

with a big red square sign

on the front and back door

announced to the world shame,

forbidden by law

to leave the house

or let anyone in. We

understood whooping cough,

could see it. Smell

in our home, the result.

One December morning

when I could take no more

of being cooped up,

of fever, coughing, vomiting blood,

no more of mother's

homemade cures

I escaped

out the back door

into family legend.

In my Dr. Dentons

flapping like a scarecrow.

barefoot. The air

was frigid enough

to glue my nostrils shut,

wind biting, snow crust knife

bloodying my thin bare shins.

Corona Virus, the King of Many Crowns

On the trail up

to the mountain I meet him

as I walk beneath

a rain shadow of spruces.

On a dark morning

I see him coming.

His small dog slipped

free from him

drags its makeshift

ribbon like a leash.

He comes nearer asks

"Know anybody

with a room to rent?

Is there a room

for any of us outside

on the street?"

We have a room

but we can't leave it

or invite you in.

The invisible king flaunting

his many crowns

forbids it.

If Our Lives the Fates Hold by a Thread

When someone says a life

or a world is hanging

by a thread we know

they speak figuratively.

No matter what you believe,

following on the heels of that

metaphor you secretly hope it's not

that fraying shoestring you keep

meaning to replace.

But whatever your phobias

or beliefs, you can only hope

that when your life or

world dangles by a thread

it's a silken spun fiber.

These Days All Cerulean Sky

Will these be our own days?
Will they always be this blue?
What makes us believe we bought
and paid for them even if

we're stone broke? Who owns
such days? We the people?
We own everything down
here or else we can buy it.

This is one time we're
all seers: next week is
September and sure dark
dark clouds and rain

weigh down the days
into next summer, down
these days the weakening
sun walking by each morning.

We're aware, pay close

attention, we know the days

are shorter, a reality we're

not eager to share with loved ones.

Where does the blue sky end?

We might as well ask

where do blue dogs go

when there are no clouds.

Days of No Sky

Every morning I arise

hoping to see sky.

Out my window a cliché

turned true, where there's smoke

there's fire, and all around us.

Yesterday the sun made weak

teasing shadows.

Today I imagine a patch

of pale blue sky like real estate

I bought, am still paying for.

In the evening news

silhouettes of fire

fighters stand against

 a horizon

of encroaching flames.

I look a weakened sun
right in the eye
without fear

of being blinded,
dare him to return
take back his kingdom.

Now ever nearer
smoke hides flames,
winds that fan towns,

miles of forest around
us to ash. We await
never arriving

rain to smother fire, wash smoke
cinders from the skies, wash grit
from red rimmed eyes.

Lament for Us All

I.

Enough blue

to patch a sailor's pants

is all I want as

I look up

prayerful, honoring the sky

so long absent because of smoke

from wildfires menacing for days though,

to me it seems centuries.

The planet is burning up:

on my windshield ash

but a fleck, in tearful eyes a speck

the old growth forests cremated.

Cabins, mobile homes, tract

houses consumed by the dragon.

We lament the giant trees

lost, for the people displaced,

long gone their shelter.

Where will the deer run

even if they are faster than flame?

II.

And those who can't escape?

The air is too dangerous to breathe.

Brazil: The Awkward Rhyme of Breath & Grief

I have never been there in real life.

I have been to where

the Amazon gets its start,

where the first drop of rain

from banana leaf falls

onto tropical rain forest's

floor, where our great

river of grief begins.

You have been there, perhaps

some part of you is still there,

your eyes burning from smoke

of the conflagration, on

the great shoulder of Brazil

where you stand by night's shore

of dreams, your small backpack

crammed with our sorrow.

Along with the great selva

with its gasping breath and ours,

we mourn charred totems

standing while we sift ashes

for skeletons of creatures past

endangered status: what we too

have become. Surely we must grieve

for the forest, so must it mourn for us.

A wraith of smoke weaves our

heartache with universal mourning

every bit as powerful as the sorrow

we feel for the forest. You stroll along

grey shorelines of reveries

stirring with a burnt stick

wisdom you have collected

while absent from our lives,

knowledge that can help us deal

with the catastrophes of our planet,

help us continue our lives

without you, without the mass jungle,

our lungs. Without breath we can't go on.

We await your call, your wisdom.

Praying

It's a dark gloomy morning,
Sunday. sabbath.

I prefer Sun Day
though I celebrate neither.

Slim notes
of church bells, distant thunder.

Trapped beneath the weight of clouds.
muffled sounds don't

comfort me. I walk the slope
of a dead volcano praying

for the sun to burn off
sea air, condensed fog

on the tallis over my shoulders,

to dry the wet blanket

covering my dull morning,

this padded cell.

Even the Thinnest Cloud

I didn't ask for more
than a bit of blue in the sky.
— Luis Cernuda

The cerulean sky blocks the sun

from your eyes, casts doubt, spoils

your most sparkling awakening.
The day is off to a brilliant start until

marine air invades, layering your world,

causes you to lose confidence in the sun's

power to return, burn away yesterday's

old rags these morning clouds.

One Hundred Days

In pitch black Portland
in clogged rivers of streets,

a Molotov cocktail goes awry.
Its creator, his feet aflame

like wings on Mercury's heels,
runs, flaps his arms

like a great bird
unable to achieve flight.

His fleeing fans
an all consuming fire

until he trips. Someone
not a policeman

rolls him over and over

to smother the flames,

his protest now

sparks and ashes.

Every Year a New Year an Old Year

Again on Yom Kippur
I think of all the stones
I've cast through windows
of houses of the innocent,

all the expressions of hate
that frown my face,
most of them in the mirror.
Today I write to a niece

disavowed by her father
where I accuse myself
jokingly of being less a mensch
for once, not reconciling with him.

I leave the letter overnight to cool.
Awakening I destroy it instead
of sending it, as though that
were a thin slice towards

making amends. But

in my heart I know that act

doesn't settle anything... I shred

the pages, cast them

like petals out onto next year's

already muddying flowing water.

Crush

I.

Have you been up to the top lately?
Some activists have tipped over the statue,

What do you think? Without waiting
for an answer, my neighbor says

It's getting too close to home. I say
nothing, I agree but not in the way he thinks.

II.

What is the demise of a few statues
of wrong thinking patriarchs

compared to ideas, ideals.
Don't take the statues down

with white gloves to a museum
where they are protected and hidden

until another generation resurrects them.

Take them back to the quarry

where they came from, put them

through the rock crusher, transform them

into a clean gravel pathway

where the crunch of each step reminds us

how far we have not come.

The Net Everything I Don't Need Gets Caught In

I drag a grapnel over the bottom of the world
Everything I don't need gets caught
— Tomas Transtomer

Like the trawler my nets

drag the bottom of the sea

come up with everything

I don't need:

a whale vertebra

a hatchcover, rusty

cans of leaking vegetables

from Russian factory ships.

The past is a sea

either I catch no fish

or none is edible

or like my friend's boat,

Our Lady of Fair Voyage,

on the second

drag, along with sea bed mud

and sand they brought up

so many fish

that to bring the catch aboard

would sink them.

They released the catch

back to the sea.

That's what I want

to do with my seine

of random dreams, memories.

The Truth, the Whole Truth

Claudia Rankine says of memory:
it's not the truth it's not a lie

so where does that leave me? We
aren't given permission

to select what we remember
have less control over it

than what we dream. We poets
edit our dreams

before we write them.
We labor without success

to correct our past, suffer
the barbs of our critics

— we ourselves but others as well

who insist that it

never happened. We hate them for

catching us out

making us face the past,

a wall of bricks built

with only mud for mortar.

When we are far from dreams

we pore over every painful sliver

stuck beneath our nails

that insists, keeps us from sleep;

each detail of a life we managed

to stumble though and come out

on the other side into a less than perfect

present. We punch our pillows

not to get more comfortable

but to get a better view.

Stowaway

I.

Behind him Brooklyn Navy Yard.
He waves farewell to Lady
Liberty thinking only
of the twelve day sea voyage ahead.

A breather at Norfolk with a dry eyed
final goodbye to the USA, then
on to Hatteras and gale force winds,
into steaming Cuba.

At Guantánamo he gives hardly
a second thought to his Navy time:
he quit it to enlist
in the army for a faster getaway.

As the troopship slices down
through obsidian Caribbean seas

he watches the night sky open, hopes

to spot the mythical Southern Cross,

hoping that vision reveals a glimpse

of what lies ahead as he sails

into tomorrow's flying fish, Puerto Rico,

Trinidad's steel band thunder.

II.

Four decks below the waterline

between him and the South Atlantic

is only the steel hull. He feels the

engine, the ship's heart

beat matches his own, not pounding

from fear of the unknown but

the excitement of what lies ahead.

To be out in the brisk salt night

sends him escaping the cigar

smoke and slop tides of seasick vomit,

of homecoming crap shooting

soldiers from Asia. He clambers

topside, takes hand over hand

the ratlines to the crow's-nest

atop the swinging main mast

that stirs constellations

in the inverted blackened

kettle of stars and planets.

Beneath the dizziness of dancing stars

he has time to reconsider

why he crossed the single strand

of barbed wire that kept him

from the world, why he ran away

so fast, so far from his family,

from the small country town.
Suddenly blind in the
klieg lights of Manhattan,
he creeps into dim smoky bars

days before boarding the ship.
Though a passenger, he slips
in and out of shadows
like a stowaway. In innocence

he considers the proposition
of the drunk sailor who
wants to trade places, offers
him a blow job if he'll take the bow

lookout at 4 bells. With each island
he takes a further giant step
away from his old life.

III.

Unaware that as he sails ever nearer

the Equator, his life is changing

forever. Nearing the end of the journey,

proud of his hard-earned sea legs

he's an old salt at the port rail

dreamily reading Richard Dana's

Two Years Before the Mast

while beneath the keel

the crude- oil-black Orinoco

slides into the Caribbean.

Saluting Venezuela's

paling emerald shoreline he

leaves his years green

as the jungle behind, sails on

into the Dragon's Mouth.

Siesta Dream

At the mouth of the Orinoco

a shrimp fisherman in a cayuco

casts his butterfly net wide

onto coal black waters, sifts

three diamonds fallen last night

from the Southern Cross.

Memory Whore

You can't own my memories
they are like sacred ground
you can't buy them unless
the gods agree. You can

squat there, rent them.
I set the rate, charge
as much as I want. You can't
edit or correct them.

It's not up to you to
establish what is true,
what's false. My memory
like history is the biggest liar.

But it's poetry, don't forget!
If my memories are not the same
as yours, tough. I'm not liable
for them. I'm the memory whore

so pay me the going rate,

sue me, or shut the fuck up.

Doppelganger

As I walk the shadowed leafy lane,
wobbling toward me: A stick figure,
a ballerina, a crucifixion. An auk
failing to achieve flight.

Every fifty paces he stretches
his arms, bows, squawks:
Hi! I'm Barbara Walters. If it's not
one thing it's another . . . Hi I'm . . .

Yesterday I saw him again
walking like a monk bowed
to silence, his lips moving
bowed like the rest of us

on our morning walk
in line, making our clock
wise rounds. With each step
we reinvent ourselves.

Counting Crows

A single crow is an omen of bad luck.
Finding two means good luck.
Four crows means wealth.
Five crows means sickness is coming.
Six crows means death is nearby.

Crows in a long line south

at the edge of the reservoir

bathe happily we suppose,

not used to seeing them

take their ablutions so publicly.

Little do they realize

how few hours are left until sunset.

Not concerned are they about

how along the horizon to the south

the sun rolls then drops fast like blinds;

how few days remain

of a year dark

as wet black satin feathers

shiny as lacquered boxes

in the sunlight.

There are as many deaths

carefully tallied up at the end of

each day as crow feathers.

I don't count precisely

the number of crows

splashing along the shore,

past number six is only foreboding.

What am I to make of the crow

feathers strewn on my

calendar's remaining days?

Downhill from the Park

A seasoned man sits in a folding

chair, at a folding table, with

a thermos open, a leather

book to read or write in.

A fraying straw hat

he surveys the timber

hills that guard the ocean.

One supposes a painter

but there is no easel in sight.

The only color a red

Irish setter in the grass.

Without warning it leaps up, flees

downhill to the flat below.

A pileated woodpecker flies

back to its nest, goes in

to feed its restive brood.

Over the past five years I

watched the fir tree die

become a snag, watched

the woodpecker carve a nest,

at its door saw tiny open beaks.

I watch the elder too as he persists,

comes each day, as the birds

flash by, as shadows grow.

In Memoriam

– *Marvin, Peter, Vern*

In a December midmorning

closed in as dim evening

I get the news: a Bell's last toll.

They go everyday

those surrounding me,

my old playmates

some younger, some

older as I stand guard

on the last ice floe.

In water warming

beneath my feet, the floe

wafer thin, melts, and drifts south.

St Vitus Danse

– ye Panademick of June 24, 1374

We deed our parte

In our ecstasy drunk

All the leather tankards

Ours & theirs

Watched blossums

Swirling grew insane w' jelasee

Dansed with them 'til we dropt

& the winde ded quit

We loste the danse

& faine woode lie downe

Til the winde woode cum backe

We drifted wee thistle downs stolen

By the winde to dreem

In our boozee-snooze.

When we woke

The tankards of meade

We had stolen were emptee

As were our deeds

Of fantasee

II.

Hoofprint on an Echo

Fading Half Notes in a Siesta

An exotic aroma creeps

up stairs on notes

of a mysterious song

you're humming. It's

Soup. The Musical.

A one woman show.

If you come lilting

up the stairs bearing a bowl

please don't reveal the name

of the song, of the soup.

Ask me to close my eyes.

Abandon me again to

mystery of aroma, mystery

of harmony between us.

Near Lorca in Spain

In a shadowy night,

two tricorns, disguised as ravens

atop two heads, above two visages.

Four coals of eyes become

the Guardia Civil suddenly

watching our group of six.

We sit at a table, our faces lit

by a gas lantern, a bottle of rum.

These ravens, let's call them,

suspect insurrection

these Franco nights, or more

likely cigarette smuggling,

the lantern signals

to a boat offshore. If not

they want to know

what we're doing here

at midnight on the patio

of a closed taberna whose owner

gave up, left us with a bottle

and the lamp hours ago.

Two fishermen drinking

with us mumble nothing.

I vouch for the rest of us

me, my partner, two tourists

we met earlier and we know nothing

about. In their innocence

they don't fear Civil Guards.

We're here to finish this rum

I might say but instead

offer some of it, pass them

a last pack of Swiss Marlboros.

The Guards refuse, wait wordless

hoping for a better offer

but I play dumb, all the time

trying to read the silence

of the fishermen's expressions.

They study their hands, hide

behind a story I fabricate.

Pickpocket at the Gate of the Sun

He knifed through the crowd,

a slender breeze through a bamboo grove,

hardly rattling the trees. I felt a bump.

When he started around me I seized him.

He was thin as any of the canes

in the moving grove. I shook him

like the tree that he was until

all the leaves fell to the ground

and with them my wallet.

For a moment before I released him

I held him like a long lost brother

by the shoulders, digging

deep into his obsidian eyes.

Then I gave him back his shiv,

let him go, even though the wind

whistled *policía,* watched him flee

back into the restless moving bosk

at the Gate of the Sun.

Into Journey's Eye

I stop in the alley outside

the Jamaica Café bend

pick up a corroded centimo.

Franco's head is still there

face down on the cobbles.

A feather falls from one

of the hundred pigeons

in the plaza, scattered

skyward to the cornices

of encroaching buildings.

The loss of one feather

will not deter a pigeon in

its flight, prevent its circling back.

The Guardia Civil sweeps away

refugee peddlers of cheap CDs

who take flight like pigeons.

Like the birds they'll circle

back once the police move on.

In his hurry to escape one

seller abandons a cloth

no bigger than a prayer

rug, on it a brass wedding ring.

Slight worn kneeprints

say a barefoot someone

facing east, is praying.

Outside my second story

barred windows of day

break the last man

crosses the plaza, the last

note of a flamenco

guitar floats up. But for rain,

clouds, sun would splash

gold over the Puerta del Sol,

where this morning or tomorrow

wherever you travel to, you'll start

counting, always remember

your steps away from

this point into journey's eye.

Hoofprint on an Echo

> *A horse galloping away leaves its hoofprint on the echo*
> — Rafael Alberti

I think therefore I am only

goes so far . . . I believe

he exists who walked

away uninjured from the

United DC 8 that crashed

in the woods short of the runway

in Portland. I believe he

abandoned the other

survivors, gathered up and

counted in light falling

snow though he wasn't aboard

the plane, wasn't

returning from New York.

He was never there,

according to his wife.

Lir

The sun slides away
into the horizon's cur-
tains dragging with it
tide and grey clouds.

One last hard wink:
dripping a half-drowned
surfer board pulled
from beneath him

somewhere out there
splashes his way here,
an unknown shore.
Flaming red beard,

salt rimmed eyes, he
jolts across my view.
His sea bleached
Levis, knees gone

holes the tide

can walk through.

He tramps the sea-

grapes metaphor

for a thirst

he can't drown.

Homesick

The truth is, like all places in the past,
it cannot be found any longer. There is no way
to get there.
      — Niall Williams

At this time in my life

I am painfully heart-

sick for those places

that no longer exist

or never were. Recently

My house in Maine is gone

Two years ago I meant to

drive by the old salt box

when I was near Orono

but didn't. The snap

shot I have of it enough

to trigger nostalgia.

The little square box

of a house where I was born,

where my grandfather died,

I still have pictures of.

Then there's the Ireland that

I miss more and more, an

Ireland that no longer exists.

Each trip home I search

but it eludes me I fly over the Atlantic,

savoring last glimpses of

that emerald postage stamp island.

Dodge

I don't exist before the Seventies.
I've done everything

but sand off my fingerprints.
Decades back I whited-out data

of yellowing papers lost in long banks,
filing cabinets in lightless dank

basements of erased shadows.
The beam of your flashlight

won't help you find my name.
You'll get the wrong person.

I had a very common name
in two very common languages

Have you ever been arrested?
No proof of that . . . *Been in jail?*

I refuse to answer, there's no
evidence, no record, not even

of the back alley bust
in Nogales, Sonora.

I've no distant dim Eden
to return to, little nostalgic longing.

Oh there's plenty of memory
alright but it's what I spent

all these years escaping from,
trying to forget no place I'd want to be.

When I first arrived here, wherever *here* is,
the others did nothing

but talk about going "back home."
How long has it been? they asked.

Country songs are full of it: *Missouri,*
(anywhere) *I Hear You*

Calling . . . Well that phone number
is disconnected, no longer in service.

When you ask where I'm from
I have only a feeble response:

my past is a phantom limb
that in longest of sleepless nights

aches for a place, a past I've never known.

Layers

> *I have walked through many lives;*
> *some of them my own.*
>   — Stanley Kunitz

I have walked down city

side streets whose names

are best forgotten, staggered

up cul-de-sacs where humanity

sleeps beneath its rags. I thought

the sleepers blind, as I was blind.

No hope of ever seeing

light again but I staggered on

back into the few yellow street

lights still burning, I half crawled back

to some scarred mahogany bar of

lives, of faces blank, empty black

alleys, eyes blind curtains. I didn't

judge, hope they don't judge me.

I say: I'm not who I was then.

They don't buy it.

Customs

In Keflavik at 1 a.m. with eyes
burned from lack of sleep

we watch the sun dim,
circle the bruised horizon.

We try in vain to follow it,
wait for it to go down.

A curtain lidded eye, meticulous
as an immigration officer,

the sun counts each of us
as we file to the Paris plane.

Drinking from Sunset's Cup

We sat there in Deia

drinking up the

last bittersweet drops

of our cocktails

on the patio

outside Graves'

place on the cliff, fighting

over the sunset

over the Mediterranean

over unseen wars in the Middle East

over the rights

the wrongs

of their struggles, ours.

Mousiki

Our dream of sitting in an outdoor cafe

on a cliff above the crater sipping ouzo

or Greek coffee to the strains of a bouzouki

became headache disco each dark Santorini night.

When we complained, our landlady urged us

to go hear "The sweet singing" of the nuns

in the Dominican Convent in nearby Fera.

Sweet indeed and harmonious, a soothing

choir but not traditional Greek music.

We fled to Athens yet hoping to find *mousiki*

found only Easter at the foot of the Acropolis.

In the village-like Plaka we gave over our dream

at dinner to insistent mewlings from the shadows

of feral cats.

Describing Our Fate

Talking aloud to ourselves repeating the words
That are always used to describe our fate.
                                        — Mark Strand

We thought ourselves clever

Our first full day in Athens

finding our way here

from the nightmare

of the evening before where

our door into the hall

wouldn't lock but we were

not murdered by ouzo drinkers

in the small lobby bar

of a hotel so disreputable only

taxi drivers knew its code

name "good hotel my cousin's."

At the train station we stood

for an hour, but for a rumpled

stranger we'd be there still

Amerikanós, he called out,

The train doesn't come

here anymore, pull those tags

from your luggage, put the map

away, try not to look

the way you look, they'll know

In this part of the city

you are helpless. Take a taxi,

mine, he smiled.

Down the Path from Imerovigli

To the seaward side of

this mesa our

throats dry as the

gaping whispering fish

mouths of abandoned caves

we came to a small cistern.

From a thread hangs

a tin dipper

in English a note:

Our only hope

on this island is rain

If you are thirsty drink

but not too much

And do not pour

your leftover water

back into the well.

Through dusty portholes

behind the heavy door

inside the washed

white Theoskepasti Chapel

a seven day candle

burns all the way to Easter.

Back up the slope

a single red poppy

bleeds a spearpoint

wound in the side

of lonely Skaros.

Swimming Through My Thoughts

Today on St Johns Eve
on the West Coast of Ireland
I think of Emma as she swims
out from the other shore

into this same Atlantic
challenging the sea god Lir.
As the sun sets in Brazil
it's the Festa de São Jão.

Here it's the traditional night
for bonfires, for first river
swims, time to challenge
Boann, goddess of the Boyne,

Sinann, goddess of the Shannon.
But Lir was the greater challenge.
Emma swam alongside him until he
folded her in his arms, stole her away.

Pocket Change

We search beneath thunder
of ocean waves for perfect sand
dollars then without a thought
drop them back into shallow

tide pools of our pockets.
Up in the cabin we're shocked
at the destruction: once perfect
dollars now pieces and bits.

Two bits, four bits
six bits, a dollar: they chanted
in Grandfather's time
when coins were broken

into bits, fragments counted
out as though on velvet.
We still say breaking a dollar
though it is paper

when we want change.

A penny, a dime, a quarter

lost from anyone's pocket

on the street, worth-

less as bits of broken shell.

Because of a Few Escudos

– for Christopher Howell

I thought of jumping from

the cab, trudging back

up the hill, to ask the marble

tombstone of Luis Camões

for his advice. Because the poet

had one love, one life

and wrote one poem.

Because I wanted to ask him

how to deal with this

rollicking epic taxi ride.

For even in my inebriated state

I gotta write something

about this kept coming

back to me, the way my mind

writes in dreams, in drink.

His one poem was enough

to assure Camões's immortality.

Couldn't my attempt do

the same? My ego shot through

alcohol soaked reasoning

not even the drinks could

quench my desire to immortalize

this adventure. Because

we screamed up and down

the San Francisco-like

hills of Lisbon. Portugal

at midnight after his absinthe

and mine as we swerved

through slick darkened streets,

after sharing a bottle I saw

as literary, knew I would fail.

The liquor that drove

Rimbaud crazy and because

it might have been his death

and might have been mine too.

By then the ride was too fast,

too exhilarating, no time

for my blurry life

to pass before my eyes.

The cabbie driving

like crazy not slowing

because as we careened

down hills, he sped up

to achieve the next ones

as he rehearsed the life

of a cousin in San Diego.

Because after a long pull

from the bottle the cabbie

handed to me and because

we drank the health

of Lusitania's crown jewel

with the last few drips

from the tipped bottle:

a telescope through which

the moon was barely visible.

Wells of Marnay

The wells beside each house

are filled, have become

quaint flower boxes.

The Seine nearby grows

green to brown,

no hope of potable water.

Ah! We are not in the desert,

it rains here though

not often in summer.

Where are the deep wells

of yesterday, where

all the moons are captive?

In the courtyard of the Mairie

in a pyramid of plastic,

water bottles are empty, silent

even as at the Assumption

Church electronic bells

cast out the hours.

Fishing for Time

Life is not lost by dying;
life is lost minute by minute . . .
in all the thousand small uncaring ways.
— Stephen Vincent Benét

We never notice a speck of dust as a second,

nor motes small as atoms even as we watch them

climb the ladder of light, the sun our microscope.

Whether it's swept up, mopped up

or blown away by blustery

winds it's gone like sound

disappearing down the road

from a T Bird we never owned

in youth or old age,

or that handful of dust

we toss over our shoulder

for good luck.

Exactly

We stand exactly where the moon
at midnight cuts flowing obsidian

in half. The two strips of the river
wave like long black satin ribbons.

I dive from the cliff, bring them back
for you to tie up your dark tresses.

Streamers disappear in your hair
until the glimmering moon soon weaves

back through night's deep forest.

ACKNOWLEDGEMENTS

Some of these poems were first published in *World to Come* and *Praxis Magazine of Art and Literature*.

SPECIAL THANKS

I would like to thank Karen Checkoway, my best reader.

My children and grandchildren are always a source of delight and inspiration. They keep my spirits afloat and my poetry flying.

I am grateful for all my friends, colleagues, and mentors who have encouraged me over the years: Tom Bremer, Henry Carlile, Jim Carmin, Philip Garrison, Michele Glazer, Sam Green, Henry Hughes, John Laursen, Sandra McPherson, Paulann Petersen, Chip Phillips, Jennifer Richter, Keith Scribner, Laurie Sheck, Greg Simon, Lisa Steinman, Jim Shugrue, Clem Starck, Sandra Williams, and Patricia and Vince Wixon.

I thank my publishers Christopher Howell (Lynx House Press), Christine Holbert (Lost Horse Press), Jessie Lendennie (Salmon Poetry), Karunesh Kuma Agauwar (Cyberwit), Bob Durand (Yes! Press), Nelson Ball (Weed/flower Press), and D.R. Wagner (Runcible Spoon), who have stood with me over the years presenting poetry to the world.

Most of these poems were written during the COVID-19 Pandemic of 2020-21. Though the year seemed like a decade, my neighbors brightened the pathway through the darkness. They know and appreciate what I do, and this sense of community carried over into my work as a poet. I would especially like to thank Jane Ames, Nancy Ketrenos, Freddy and Roger Lunt, Gretchen and James Rowell, and Gretta Grimala.